SERIES EDITORS

Dr. Sally Monsour
*Georgia State University
Atlanta*

Mary Jarman Nelson
*Music Consultant
Winter Park, Florida*

Music in Open Education

by Sally Monsour

*Professor of Music Education
Georgia State University
Atlanta*

Classroom Music Enrichment Units

The Center for Applied Research in Education, Inc.
521 Fifth Avenue, New York, N.Y. 10017

© 1974

The Center for Applied
Research in Education, Inc.
New York

Library of Congress Cataloging in Publication Data

Monsour, Sally.
   Music in open education.

   (Classroom music enrichment units ₍1₎)
   "Useful teaching/learning resources": p.
   1. School music—Instruction and study—United
States. 2. Open plan schools. I. Title. II. Series.
MT3.U5M63   780'.72973   74-2238
ISBN 0-87628-214-1

Printed in the United States of America

About Music in Open Education

This handbook is an introduction to teaching music in an open, or "informal," classroom, This implies that children are allowed to grow at their own developmental pace. It means that a child's musical experience contains a large share of creative opportunity and self-initiated discovery. Most of all, it means that structured, goal-oriented lessons are based on contemporary ideas of a child's total development.

The environment in this type of education is positive, reinforcing, and full of exciting possibilities. The teacher places value on flexibility and the free exchange of musical ideas while trusting children to make decisions and work with classroom materials on their own. Songs and pieces are selected with as much imagination as possible, keeping in mind the natural interests of young children. Also, the authenticity of music is maintained so that the elements that make up music become the most important. In this way, children can experience what it is like to be a composer, performer, conductor, or critic. This experience becomes real and interesting through direct music-making, active listening, and original musical thinking.

The ideas and lessons in this handbook include making the transition from a traditional program to one that is open and flexible. Individualization of musical activities is stressed and typical examples are included. Ideas for the physical arrangement of space are also given. There are important suggestions for building rapport between teacher and students, and avoiding sound competition problems that sometimes arise in the flexible use of space for music-making purposes. Interspersed throughout are illustrations of activity-lessons that have been developed and tested for use in open classrooms. These consist of project proposal ideas, learning packages, contracts, job cards, and other small-group activities.

Finally, this handbook is based on the developing notion that the principles of open education are currently being tested and applied in many different types of schools and classrooms. Because of this, the teacher should look forward to the challenge of creating solutions according to the needs of his or her particular school or community. Some helpful guidelines are included here, but the ultimate goals of an authentic program can best be met by the teacher who has studied the basic literature on the philosophy of open education. Several sources for this purpose are included at the end of the handbook in the section *Useful Teaching/Learning Resources.*

Hopefully, the well-prepared teacher in open education will be able to structure continuity into a child's experiences with music so that goals will be met that will, in turn, affect his entire life. Teachers could make a good start in this direction if they would recall their own best experiences with interesting or beautiful music, and then plan lessons children can enjoy—all taking place in a free, yet disciplined, environment.

Sally Monsour

Contents

*The environment we seek to create within the school
is one which is truly responsive to the needs and
interests of children; in which children's learning is
deeply rooted in experience; where knowledge becomes
important because it is relevant and put to use; and
where children, in an atmosphere of mutual trust and
respect, can carry on with each other and with adults
the kind of open dialogue that is the
essence of good education.*[1]

— — David E. Armington

1

Creating Open Environments for Music

The teaching/learning environment in open education runs the entire gamut of the "Where," "How," "With What." The "Where" concerns the physical and social setting of the class. The "How" includes the processes and techniques of learning. The "With What" are the media and materials used for gathering together experiences and information.

Each of these factors falls into place once the auditory goals of music in open education are understood. For example, children may work individually on some activities, but will need other people to perform in musical ensembles. Some children may use structured discussion to tell about their musical ideas. Others may not have the musical vocabulary for this.

Musical experiences require concentration on aural resources for musical performance and listening. The sound factor becomes important. Because of this, the Commission on Open Space Schools of the American Association of School Administrators recently reported that there should be special areas designated for music within open-space constructions.[2] Also within this space there should be equipment for individual and small-group listening stations, in addition to traditional instruments, such as piano, drums, bells, autoharps, and so on.

---

[1]David E. Armington, "A Plan for Continuing Growth," from *Open Education,* ed. Ewald Nyquist and Gene R. Hawes. (New York: Bantam Books, 1972, pp. 67-68.)

[2]*Open Space Schools.* Report of the American Association of School Administrators (Washington, D. C. 1972), pp. 16, 45.

Arranging the Physical Environment

In planning facilities for music in open education, the important thing is that teachers look at the whole environment and make decisions about the flexible use of space for musical activities. These should include many things to do and places to be. Some schools have experimented with using the entire school environment in musical ways. While some of these are functional, they do provide activities for the "odd" moments children experience in open-school environments. Sometimes they provide the "spark" that sends a child down a path of considerable musical validity.

Some examples are:

1. Hang a large branch in the corridor (or school entrance) with the challenge to attach musical objects and symbols in mobile style. These are frequently changed by the children to include sound sources, wind chimes, rustling papers, etc.
2. Place a set of melody bells in the media center or in another central school area. Include a message such as: "Play your favorite tune on these bells. Make up your own."
3. "Prepare" an autoharp by putting scraps of paper, bits of wire, or paper clips among and in between the strings. Put it in the media center, or other central area, with a large sign: "How many sounds can this instrument make? Sign your name if you tried. Do you want to learn more about 'prepared' instruments? Go to the music center area and listen to the cassette called 'John Cage and His Music.'

The use of space for both individualization and ensemble performance must be flexible. There should be places within the music area for children to work alone or at listening stations. Musical resources including sound-producing instruments (both pitched and nonpitched) should be within easy access. For this purpose, there are especially designed sound space units that are now commercially available.[3] However, many teachers substitute inexpensive ways to absorb the sound and also provide for student privacy. These ideas include:

— Egg cartons or carpet scraps on the sides of bookcases placed on three sides of a small area.

---

[3]Commercial sound space units are available by companies such as Wenger Corporation, 573 Park Drive, Owatonna, Minnesota, 55056. Included in their current catalog are sound centers, modules, and portable carpeted raised platform areas for performing purposes.

— Burlap, old stage curtains, or drapes hung over the sides of study carrels, portable screens, or dividing units.

Regardless of the limitations, use suggestions from the children as well as your own imagination in making the school environment a rich source for musical involvement.[4]

Shaping the Psychological Environment

If we were to summarize what is labeled "open education," we would continually hear terms such as "flexible" and "individual." They refer to a type of learning and teaching that have always been important, but today they are being reiterated and practiced in exciting new ways. Several elements of this "openness" would be:

1. Open to the changing and developing nature of childrens' musical interests.
2. Open to the individual child's learning level.
3. Open to childrens' feelings and emotions.
4. Open to the nondirective roles of the staff.
5. Open to the direct involvement of parents.
6. Open to variety and change in room arrangement.
7. Open to activities that are distributed rather than centralized.
8. Open to the learner's own evaluation of work and behavior.
9. Open to the child's total environment as affecting his learning.
10. Open to spontaneity in day-to-day routines.

These ideas can be incorporated into the music program by teachers who are responsive and sensitive. This requires less attention to habit and fixed classroom patterns and more attention to spontaneity and new interests. When this is accomplished, the classroom avoids becoming a "still life," and becomes instead a living, creative learning space.

Adopting Open Attitudes and Behaviors

Implementing the ideas of open education requires one basic ingredient—a teacher who "feels" good about having children work independently or in small groups. This attitude goes

---

[4]Anyone interested in a full treatment of the supportive requirements for a total, well-balanced music program should consult: *Guidelines in Music Education: Supportive Requirements* (1972), prepared by the National Council of State Supervisors of Music, and available from the Music Educators National Conference, 1201—16th Street, N.W., Washington, D.C. 20036 ($1.00 per copy).

hand-in-hand with the teacher whose own personal job satisfaction does not depend upon continual direct teaching of the authoritarian type.

This aspect of teacher readiness is mentioned over and over by those who have worked in open education. They have repeatedly emphasized the need for teachers who can assume a nondirective role in at least some phases of the program. In fact, the unique personality of the teacher often becomes the most important emerging element in an open classroom.

The teacher, either individually or as a team member, carries the responsibility for planning the projects and instructional ideas for individual learning centers. This takes the time traditionally devoted to planning lessons delivered to the entire class at once. In other words, it simply is not true that in open education the teacher can relax and let the children "do" what they want to do. If and when this kind of program is allowed to exist, it will probably be unsuccessful. Teachers must prepare materials, present ideas, guide instruction, help individuals who are not self-motivated, and evaluate the progress of children and the program as a whole.

The following outlines the abilities teachers should aim for. They are not presented in any order of importance. They are all important.

The teacher should be able to:

1. Accept all levels of musical interest.
2. Plan musical experiences in flexible ways, using a variety of musical resources and materials.
3. Assimilate various musical styles into the curriculum.
4. Respect children on different musical achievement levels.
5. Adjust musical plans and prepared materials to changing situations.
6. Respond to the behavior of children in a reinforcing way.
7. Prepare musical experiences so that each child will be interested in something.
8. Use "friendly" persuasion as a directional behavioral tool.
9. Determine the atmosphere in which firmness is required.

In line with the above, the factor of self-motivation must be kept in mind. Some children cannot act freely and responsibly for long periods of time. This is not always due to teacher failure, but is one more illustration of individual differences. Children who do not tend toward self-motivation can often be responsible for short periods while needing help and direction on a one-to-one basis at other times. The needs of these children reinforce the idea of differentiated staffing and the use of part-time volunteers.

The important role of the teacher is summed up in the following excerpt from an article by Skip Ascheim entitled, "Are You Really Ready for Open Education?"

The structure of the curriculum, of the room itself, is no longer handed down from on high; it derives from the needs and interests of the people in the class. The teacher is asked to respond to 25 or 30 different individuals. Nothing is given, everything is possible. Instead of being a relay transmitter between the curriculum designer and the child, restricted to dreaming up a new way to teach fractions each year, the teacher is asked to be what, in fact, she or he is—a living being with interests and joys and fears and angers and sympathies and ideas—a person.[5]

It would be foolish to assume that all teachers can ideally fulfill all of the requirements for a music program labeled as "open." In the first place, we are not absolutely sure what all of the attributes or attitudes would be. In the second place, each teacher possesses a unique set of characteristics that will determine the classroom environment—whether formal or informal, traditional or open. Teachers who cannot accept the premises of open education would probably do a far better job to maintain a strong program in which their teaching and musical strengths can become operative than to adopt ideas in order to "keep up with the times." Such teachers should be honestly aware of their teaching talents and personal attributes. They should also try to learn about current teaching trends—their pros and cons.

Building Rapport with Children

Even in an informal environment where movement around the room is expected and encouraged, children will test their freedom in many ways. This is especially true of older children who are in a transitional situation, and who are not used to mak-

---

[5]Skip Ascheim, "Are You Really Ready for Open Education?" *Scholastic Teacher* (December 1972) pp. 3-10. This article also contains suggestions for making musical instruments.

ing choices among activities, especially those that are sound-competing.

Teachers are sometimes overly disturbed by noise or movement in the classroom and will find this aspect of open education the most distressing. They admit that their authority and control become limited. The following excerpt by Herbert Kohl contains an important point relative to the feelings of the teacher as well as the children.

Freedom can be threatening to students at first . . . They will have to test the limits of the teacher's offer, see how free they are to refuse to work, move out of the classroom, try the teacher's nerves and patience. It is not easy for the teacher either. Freedom in the classroom means freedom for the teacher as well as the students . . . If you are angry with a student . . . for refusing to do what you want him to do, tell him and try to deal with the question of why you are angry. Only when a teacher emerges as another person in the classroom can a free environment based upon respect and trust evolve. Moreover, if the teacher remains a silent, abused witness to student authoritarianism, a time will come when the teacher has had enough and will take back the freedom offered the students.[6]

Teachers have described many practical ways to deal with behavior in open education. Foremost is the notion that rules must exist and should evolve rather than be imposed. In this way, children can relax and concentrate on their activities without worrying about the reprimands of the teacher.

For example, in one music situation the noise and sound factors were beginning to disturb the children as much as they were the teacher. After an analysis of the musical composition that a small group had composed, the teacher commented: "The piece was not up to your abilities. You can usually work out something that hangs together a little better." To which the children replied, "We just couldn't hear each other." With this cue, the entire group decided on two classroom rules: "Listen for others," and "You must never keep anyone else from learning." This, in turn, created an atmosphere of concern in which individual child-

---

[6]Herbert Kohl, *The Open Classroom* (New York: The New York Review, 1969). This paperback is available in most bookstores, especially on college campuses. It should be read as an introduction to open education by any teacher who expects to work in this kind of program.

ren set about to help each other with sound problems. Summing up this type of regulatory behavior is a written notice that appeared on the chalkboard of an open classroom which read: "We are all two things: someone special and different; and someone belonging to others."

Structuring for Positive Student Behavior

The negative behaviors children exhibit can sometimes be avoided. Ideas to solve this problem range all the way from the teacher's attitude to student involvement. The following are suggestions that successful teachers have mentioned:

1. Be *ready* to accept some lack of order and messiness without acting too anxious or hostile.
2. Begin to assume there will be sound competition problems in music and be able to analyze which sounds are productive and which are not. (Quick ways to check if the sound level is disturbing: Are the children absorbed, concentrating? Are they accomplishing their set task?)
3. "Imagine" the situation and especially "imagine" yourself as a child in the situation before applying any punishment.
4. Discuss the fact that everyone works differently and is interested in different things at different times. This can be exhibited by such remarks as: "I know some of you may not be as interested in this as . . ."
5. Be sure the children are secure about the teacher's availability; that help will be forthcoming on a one-to-one basis if needed.
6. Establish the idea that children will *not* be under constant surveillance by being "watched" and "questioned" as they move about the room to get supplies, look for a special instrument, and so on.
7. Know each child as an individual. (This is easier when you see them function in a small group.)
8. Group children carefully for long-term projects or activities. Put different personalities together and be aware of children who behave negatively when put in close proximity. Put them in different groups where each will become involved in the activity rather than in the disruptive actions of a friend.
9. Make sure the children clearly understand the primary behavior rule of "not disturbing others or preventing them from

learning," and that the result of doing this is removal from the group.

10. Avoid using reprimand. Keep an atmosphere of acceptance and kindness even when being firm.

11. Be aware of musical activities in which individual children may fail and be ready to step in and repair their self-concept before they become sufficiently frustrated to become disruptive. This sometimes happens in such areas as lack of coordination when playing an instrument or inadequacy in singing.

One of the major ideas of open education is that children develop positively in a secure and enthusiastic environment. In successful "open" situations, one notices that children begin to regulate their own behavior. They learn how to come forward when shy, or how to retreat when they are imposing on others. This usually develops when the teacher does not act "interfering," but is always standing by in a helpful, resourceful role.

When children feel secure, they tend to openly assume their natural roles. Leaders will emerge, and so will followers. One hears such comments as: "Have Mike start us out, I don't like to do it," or "Tell Bob to ask Mr. Forrest to listen to our piece, he talks better than any of us." Another illustration is a very shy girl who previously showed no initiative and who began to gain confidence when she did not feel threatened. This girl began to ask for chances to "be on stage" when, after watching others conduct the original pieces of the group she was in, she whispered very quietly to the teacher, "I believe I want to be the next conductor." Her comment was so quiet that it was hardly audible. In fact, if the teacher had not been alert to individuals, it could have gone unnoticed.

Another behavior that sometimes emerges is that children begin recognizing the whole group endeavor rather than clammering for personal recognition. This, in turn, allows them to be freer in working toward the tasks in which they are occupied. For example, in a demonstration of songs and instrumental selections for parents, a small group of ten-year-olds seldom referred to the names of individual children, nor were they particularly interested in personal recognition. They consistently and voluntarily described their roles by saying, "Our group would like you to hear . . . " or "We would like to play . . . ." Even when called upon to give their names, they said, "We just all did it together." Their chief interest seemed to be the music and its performance.

In summary, it is important to analyze the reasons for the behaviors children show. When the behavior is negative or indifferent, reasons often stem from ineffective planning, unclear direction or structure within experiences, or from an alienating environment that has somehow developed.

A sensitivity toward the role played by structure
in fostering creative behavior will probably be the
most critical single determinant in establishing
creative environments . . . structure and creativity are
not antithetical to one another
but are intimately related.[1]

— — Margery M. Vaughan

2

Making the Transition from Formal to Open Music Program

The most enthusiastic and successful teachers in open education warn against plunging in too quickly without orientation. Considerable planning is needed to cross the bridge from a formal classroom to one that is more adaptive to musical preferences. This is especially true at the upper learning levels where children have had little experience working alone or in small groups.

In-service for Teachers

In most cases, transitional experiences are more crucial for the teaching staff than for the children. Unless the teacher had just come out of a successful training program with experience in individualized techniques and practices, he or she probably feels most secure in situations that have been consistently reinforcing from a personal point of view. Even though many children have benefited in the classrooms of such teachers, there are many ideas to be found in open education that could improve what was felt to be a "good situation."

An important first step in any transition to open education is the training of the teacher who is responsible for the music program, whether this is the music specialist or the classroom teacher. If the person in charge is a music specialist, there should be in-service opportunities for research in the philosophy and practices of open education. This should include observation of programs already in progress. If the school is committed to open education and uses team approaches to staffing large-space areas

---

[1]Margery M. Vaughan, "Cultivating Creative Behavior," *Music Educators Journal,* (April 1973), p. 37.

within the school, the music specialist should work as a team member with scheduled times for meeting.

If the music program is conducted largely by the regular classroom teacher or designated semispecialist, there should be workshops throughout the year in which current ideas are illustrated. Of special importance are experiences that directly involve children, or use video-taped sessions as models. Attention should be given to new materials, new music, and appropriate uses of ethnic music, both Western and non-Western.

Perhaps most important is practice in developing the teacher's own powers of creativity and originality. Teachers themselves could begin working in small groups to solve given musical problems requiring the use of their imaginative powers. They need to be informed of the common elements and principles of music and become updated on current terminology used in musical composition and performance.

Orienting Children

Some of the most successful "open" music programs provide substantial time for both the children and teacher to explore ideas for individual experiences, small-group projects, and types of evaluation in which children could share. Within the regular course of a somewhat traditional program, experience leading toward these goals can be incorporated. General guidelines are:

1. Notice the individual behavior of children as they enter and leave the room, raise their hands to answer, etc. Be aware of their distinctive qualities and personal characteristics. Try to determine their leadership potential for small-group work, grasp of musical ideas, degree of self-motivation, level and type of musical interest.
2. Carry on group discussions about individual and small-group projects and experience-centers. Make sure every child makes a contribution or suggestion in this area.
3. Begin involving the children in equipment operation. Build an atmosphere of trust in the manipulation of materials and decide where they should be housed for easy access to everyone.
4. Discuss and establish working rules in situations where the teacher will not "be in charge." Some examples are: "Do not

keep someone else from learning," "Put materials away when finished," "Trust each other."

5. Provide ways for children to experience moving around a space naturally. Avoid making them feel inhibited from fully using the entire space within the school learning environment.

6. Begin using older children within the school as well as parent volunteers as helpers and guiding teachers.

7. Give children practice using interaction skills between individuals and larger groups.

8. Assign conductors and musical leaders for group music-making. Ask for volunteers and begin to notice those with the most confidence as well as those who enjoy and seem to profit from such experiences.

9. Develop a common repertoire of interesting, simple songs that can be harmonized with simple chord progressions for both individual and small-group accompaniment.

Sample Lessons

In addition to the general guidelines above, there are many practical ideas that teachers can use as transitions to individualized instruction. One of the most successful involves experiences where students move out of large groups into individual or small-group experiences.[2] The following lesson outline is an illustration of this.

Sound Exploration Involving Individual and Small-group Work (7-9-year-olds)

"A Musical Walk-a-Round"

Goals

1. Sensitivity to qualities of sounds in the classroom environment.
2. Ability to distinguish primary elements of tempo (fast-slow), register (high-low), dynamics (loud-soft), and design (same-different).

Teacher Presentation to Large Group

Sit in a large circle.

"Close your eyes. Tell some ways that this sound (play) . . . ring, is different from this sound (play) . . . knock." (Repeat with shake and scrape or choose distinct sounds of your own.)

---

[2]Many lessons of this type may be found in the materials of the Contemporary Music Project and the Manhattanville Music Curriculum, available from Music Educators National Conference, 1201-16th Street N.W., Washington, D.C. 20036.

"Look around the room. Do you see any way you could make a hard sound? A scraping sound? A ringing sound? Other sounds?"

"Choose a friend . . . take a walk around the room. Find some (two?) ways to make sounds together. Come back to the circle and tell about the sounds you made around the room. Tell how they sounded and if you liked them. Tell why."

"Think about yourself. Can you make sounds by yourself? What are they? Keep thinking because there are a lot."

"Let's put some sounds together . . . fast then slow; high then low; loud then soft." (Make all kinds of sound descriptions and pieces.)

"Do you see any designs or patterns in this room? Does anything repeat? Stay the same? (light fixtures, rows of books, etc.) Find two other people and put some sounds together that would describe this room."

"Pick someone to conduct by bringing the sounds in and taking them out. Remember to have some silences just as a room has spaces."

"Either by yourself or with one other person, make up a sound piece using instruments, nontraditional sound sources, and your own self. Record it and play it for some friends. Play it for the teacher. Ask a friend to write a review of your piece and put it in your classroom newspaper."

Another practical suggestion is to begin using questioning procedures and self-directional cues. These may be contained on prerecorded materials with directions for individual responses. Present them to the class as a whole and discuss the results. An example might be a cassette with simple drumming patterns to which children are asked to create other rhythmic patterns or melodies. Another idea is the use of individual worksheets on which children respond on a time continuum. They must keep up and listen in order to complete the questions called for. The following is an example appropriate for very young children. It does not call for written verbal responses.

Prerecorded Lesson for Practicing Pitch
Direction of Up-Down-Same (Very Young Children)[3]

Goals

1. Practice in identification of pitch directions of up, down, and same.
2. Identification of individual child's ability to distinguish pitch directions.

---

[3] The assistance of Christine Evans, primary classroom teacher (Atlanta), in developing this material is gratefully acknowledged.

Prerecorded Script on Cassette

A worksheet (Figure 2-1) was distributed to children, and brief melodic fragments illustrating the concepts of up-down-same were played on the classroom melody bell set.

"We are going to listen to short tunes on the bells. Some will go up, some will go down, and some will stay on the same pitch. If the tune goes up, draw a circle around the arrow that goes up. If the tune goes down, draw a circle around the arrow that goes down. If the tune stays the same, draw a circle around the arrow that goes straight across. Look at your paper and put your finger on the little house. Listen to the music (tune goes up). The arrow pointing up is circled because the melody goes up. Now put your finger on the flower. Listen (tune stays on one pitch). The arrow that goes across is circled because the tune stayed on the same pitch. Now put your finger on Number 1 and draw your own circle after you hear each tune."

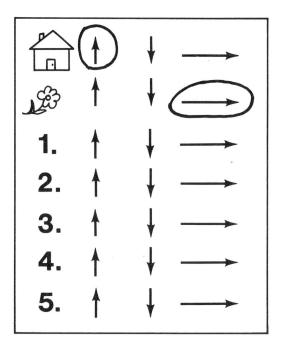

Figure 2-1

At the intermediate and upper levels, children can respond individually given written cue sheets to follow. Below is an example of a listening lesson stressing individual perception. Each child should have the Musical Plan before him.

Musical Plan

"Chester" from *New England Triptych,* William Schumann

1. Complete statement of theme (hymn "Chester") harmonized in chorale style by woodwind choir.

2. Abrupt change including percussive, rhythmic accompaniment to strident playing of theme by high woodwinds.

3. Sudden low-pitched legato accompaniment pattern by strings over pedal of "g." Theme sounding in 3rds majestically.

4. Change of mood, beginning quietly over a march rhythm played by the snare drum, which gradually increases in energy.

5. At peak of excitement, instruments "shout" closing phrase of theme followed by fragmented portions and some augmentation of theme.

6. Dramatic and sudden relaxation of energy in "lull" over orchestra followed by powerful and swift build-up leading to climactic close.

Modifying Existing Situations

Different learning levels of children will naturally require different modifying experiences in terms of transitions to open environments. Most children at the middle and upper levels may only recently have experienced situations requiring self-motivation or sharing as a team member. Teachers can begin to evaluate this by observing such skills as choice-making, awareness of others, ability to concentrate, and sound-level tolerance.

Younger children usually adapt easily to any change in the established routine. However, they require more nonverbal tools for making responses than older children who can read instructions, follow directions with more independence, and manipulate equipment. Small children can, however, *do* much more by way of individual work than we have traditionally assumed. They can turn simple equipment off and on, make written responses with pictures and shapes, evaluate with simple word usage and gesture. Also, they are capable of highly sensitive individual responses in the area of body movement and creative rhythms.

Sample Room Arrangements

In order to lead into more flexible room arrangements, teachers have modified their traditional classrooms in simple ways. These space modifications provide an intermediate step toward individualization. During this time, teachers can determine how far they can go toward breaking down larger group units. Sometimes they decide to maintain a modified approach without going beyond it. On the other hand, additional steps are sometimes taken toward the complete use of learning centers. However, the most successful programs seem to take into account the need for large group performance of music *in addition to* "centers" for individual work. In this way, a flexible room plan is maintained. Portable furniture can allow for this alteration of space according to the musical needs of different activities.

One modification scheme is to place the chairs in large semicircles (Figure 2-2). In the middle is an area carpet and a few low tables of individual or small-group work during regular classroom presentations. For this purpose, used doors can be purchased from local lumber stores for about $2.50. Bricks can be stacked under corners at convenient heights for playing instruments while sitting on the floor. The low height enables students still sitting in chairs to observe the activity. Additional, smaller centers can also be scattered around the room with sound equipment and instruments nearby. These can be used when the larger

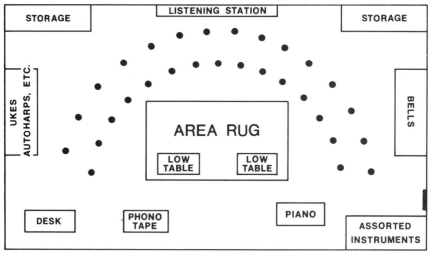

Figure 2-2

group disperses for small-group composition, listening, or discussion.

In other situations, teachers have chosen to modify their classrooms by adding perhaps one or two study centers around the room. The rest of the area is traditionally arranged with either straight rows or rehearsal-type seating plans (Figure 2-3). In this way, children can alternate by using a study center either individually or in small groups. Large-group experiences can continue to go on, especially if the study center is equipped with sound-proofing materials or listening stations.

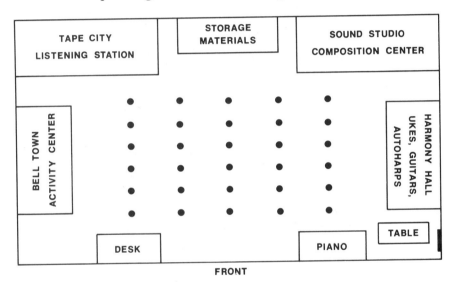

Figure 2-3

It is not enough merely to respect childhood; it is necessary to respect children as well, which means respecting students' individuality, their needs, their strengths, their weaknesses. This means valuing individual differences instead of seeing them as a problem.[1]

— — Charles E. Silberman

3

Individualizing the Music Program

Individual instruction means that the person who is learning must do the work required in order to learn. For this reason, there are as many ways of planning for individual experiences as there are children.

Music-making can include all of the experiences through which children can learn independence, self-organization, and

---

[1]Charles E. Silberman, ed., *The Open Classroom Reader* (New York: Random House, 1973), p. xix.

self-motivation. It also allows each child to cooperate with others in achieving a group aim, in listening, and in communicating. Even though these may not be strictly musical goals, they tend to radiate from an interesting, well-designed music program. They may also be important in the development of sensitive persons, able to express themselves in artistic ways.

The guidelines for individualizing the music program should remain somewhat flexible. They should also be well thought out. The following are some ideas to keep in mind:

1. No child should vote "no" to all activities presented for selection. If teachers observe this happening too frequently, there are probably too few interesting ideas from which to choose. In other words, every child must participate in some project or experience in music.
2. Choices of projects or activities should be sufficiently limited to avoid frustrations over making selections. There should be variety, but not overabundance.
3. All experiences should be goal-directed and the children should share in the continuing development of these goals according to their own interests and learning rate.
4. Some type of written (or concrete) project proposal (or contract) helps to give structure to open-ended experiences. Children need to have a sense of their own direction and progress.

As in other subjects, there are many labels and systems for structuring an individual music program. These include projects, packets, contracts, study units, mini-courses, job cards, and so on. But regardless of the name, the particular experience should be planned in terms of the time allotment, space, resources, and philosophy of the teacher (or team) in charge.

The following are practical examples of some of these individualized experiences as developed and used by teachers. Some are carried on within a separate music classroom, some are incorporated into clusters or other large-space areas, and some are conducted in a self-contained classroom by the classroom teacher.

Projects

Music projects are extensively used. In many ways, they are similar to traditional project instruction developed during the core curriculum days of the progressive education movement. They are interesting to children because they can expand an interest of their own. This is especially true at middle and upper levels where reading ability affords independence.

The selection and pacing of music projects are self-initiated by the child. Prior to his selection, however, the child should be familiar with the resources in the classroom as well as extensional resources outside of the school. He should know the limits for selecting a project topic and be assured that the instructional staff, teachers and helpers, are ready to help him get started and offer assistance.

Children are highly imaginative in selecting project subjects once they have become "tuned in" to the possibilities and resources. The lists below were found in open schools—the first taken from a "cluster" wall in an open space school, and the second from a self-contained music room. Naturally, the music projects on the cluster wall were included with several projects in other subjects. The second list consists of titles directly related to the music program.

Partial Project List on a Cluster Wall
1. Elephants, Their Hide and Their Pride — Jane
2. Cooking Brownies — Fred
3. Moog Synthesizer, Its Music and Its Mechanism — Jerry
4. Create a Rhythm Story — Mary, Tom, Allen

Partial Project List on the Music Area Wall
1. The Music of Japan in Song and Story — Jamison
2. Humor in Music — Gloria
3. What Is Electronic Music? — George
4. Strings—All of Them! — Laura

The most successful programs based on projects are those in which children submit a proposal before they begin. Depending on their learning level, children may either state their proposal verbally as the teacher writes it down, or the child may write his own proposal and go over it with the teacher. The following guidelines may be helpful:

Objective: Think About What You Could Do
    Child initiates an idea based on his own musical interests.
Process: Decide How You Could Do It Best
    Child poses three or four questions he will try to answer in his project.
    Child anticipates the materials he hopes to use.

Child presents his ideas to the teacher who helps him clarify his ideas and come up with a workable outline.

<u>Learning Time:</u> Decide How Long It Would Take to Get It Done

Child indicates approximate date he feels he will be ready to present his project to the group.

<u>Evaluation:</u> How Well Did You Do?

Child, class, and teacher(s) discuss reactions to the project.

Applying the preceding ideas, Mrs. John Culver, 4th-level classroom teacher, describes the following procedure. Although her class has a special music teacher, Mrs. Culver allows her children to develop projects as a part of their other activities. She characterizes her situation as a self-contained open classroom.[2]

The Use of Project Proposals

1. <u>Conference.</u> The child and teacher meet for a conference, at which time the child specifies what topic he proposes to research. The teacher serves as secretary for the transaction, writing in duplicate as the child talks. As the child verbalizes about the topic, the teacher helps by rewording, and guides by rephrasing and clarifying the questions. If the child is unable to choose some important questions (or to suggest at least three), the teacher helps with such decisions. When discussing how to carry out the research or to present the report, the teacher may have some questions that will guide the student in ways he may not have considered. Finally, a date is set on which the teacher makes it clear that this is a proposed date, and that if it isn't possible for the student to present the report at that time, an extension may be made. All proposals are then tacked up in a specified place so that all students may browse through the list and see what reports are coming up.

2. <u>Reporting.</u> Usually the proposal results in a written report of some kind. This may include pictures, graphs, illustrations, and charts. The reports are always given orally to the whole class. Since they usually cover topics of special interest to the reporter, he is able to tell the others about a body of knowledge with which they are not familiar. In the course of the report, the child may include demonstrations, films, show products resulting from the research, or introduce experts on the subject, who then add to the oral presentation. (Parents or other visitors often share their special talents.) At the conclusion of the report, it is customary for the student to ask a question about his topic. A prize

[2] I wish to express my grateful appreciation to Mrs. Culver (Westminster School, Atlanta) for her contribution to this publication.

is given to the child answering. This procedure has resulted in a higher degree of attention paid to the speaker than was given in the past.

3. Evaluation. While the student is making his presentation, the teacher writes up an evaluation, which is then given to the child. In this way, he receives an immediate reaction to his presentation and has in writing suggestions for future improvement. The evaluation sheet is headed with the student's name and the topic of the report. Next are listed strong points of the report. Finally, the weak points are listed. Not only is the content included in the evaluation of the report, but also its presentation to the children, and amount of variety, interest, and clarity. The manner of presentation is evaluated—whether or not the speaker spoke clearly, seemed to know his subject material, kept the interest of the class, spoke too long, and so on. The amount of variety has been amazing. One child in Greek costume showed photographs of his trip and illustrations taken from the body of his report. He passed around souvenirs, and finally served baklava to the entire class. A child who works with her father in his photography darkroom brought all of the paraphernalia for developing pictures and showed how she photographed, developed, blew up, and mounted her own photos. This was displayed with step-by-step charts using the actual film and prints.

Under the weak points category, it is possible for the teacher to guide the student in future presentations by pointing out things of which the student might not be aware. Usually, the strong points far outweigh the weak ones, and the students seem to accept both well.

A description of one of these projects is described below:

Mary Lee Gibson's Report (10 years of age)

Mary Lee worked on her proposal diligently for quite some time. The actual written part did not take too long, but she spent a good bit of time working with other students in the classroom who performed her compositions. She had composed two pieces that showed an understanding of the uses of different instruments. Her report had good continuity. All of the children have experience working with the Orff instruments in their music class, and transfer this skill to working with our classroom instruments. Mary Lee has made several of the instruments she describes in her report, notably an "Odds and Ends Xylophone." All the children enjoy playing it. The following is her project proposal sheet.

Project Proposal

Name: Mary Lee Gibson

Date: February 20, 1973

Proposal Topic: Percussion Instruments

Things I want to find out about my topic:

1. History of percussion instruments.
2. How to write a song using homemade and classroom percussion instruments.
3. Perform the song
   a. By myself
   b. With friends

Possible ways I might present my material:

1. Tell class how I went about writing my music.
2. Tell something of the history of percussion instruments.
3. Perform the music.

Possible field trips or special resource people I might employ in following up my topic:

Percussion players in the Atlanta Symphony.

Date of Presentation: March 7

Figure 3-1 is a reproduction of the first paragraph of Mary Lee's eight-page project.

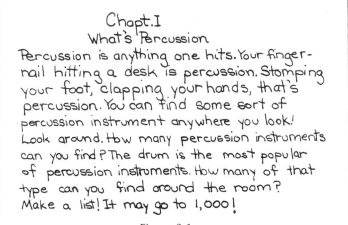

Figure 3-1

Learning Packets

Learning packets are among the most popular types of in-struction in open education. Classroom teams spend considerable time writing these packets or "mini-courses." Much thought goes into the learning sequence of each packet and the appro-priate materials and responses for varying age levels.

For primary children, responses are usually nonverbal. These may be in the form of drawings, circling, or answering on audio tape. In music, these packets should have some sound-music responses as well. Listening stations are ideal for many such packets because several students can work without compet-ing sounds. Other activities can go in the same space, such as rehearsal, instrument lessons, or individual contract work.

The following pages include three examples of learning pack-ets—one each at the upper, intermediate, and primary levels. The contents are flexible and can be adapted to various circumstances.

The first example entitled "What's the Piano All About?" is a fully developed packet for upper level students, approximately eleven to thirteen years of age. It has been used successfully in seventh grade general music classes, and requires a grand piano and instruction sheets reproduced below. The packet was written for a small group, but with some alteration in wording, it could be completed by an individual.

MUSIC LEARNING PACKET[3]
What's the Piano All About?

(Upper Level)

Welcome to the piano discovery center! Since this is a group project, you will need to cooperate with each other as much as possible every time you meet together. The piano discovery center consists of eight sections. As you com-plete each section, you will turn in to me what you have discovered. Please make every effort to understand all the material in each section. If there is something that puzzles you, ask someone in your group to help. Please re-member that Mr. Williams is available if you need his help. When you have completed the entire project, you will receive a letter grade that will be based on your individual understanding of the piano.

---

[3] This packet was developed by Mr. Marion Williams, W.A. Fountain Junior High School, Forest Park, Georgia. Used by permission.

LAST-MINUTE REMINDERS:

Cooperate.

Share.

Call on Mr. Williams when no one else in your group can answer your
questions.

Enjoy yourself.

SECTION I   SELF-DISCOVERY: JUMP IN!

Examine the piano—outside, inside, top, bottom, and at any other angle that
you can think of! Feel free to have group discussion. Make a list of the things
you find out about the piano. Please put this page in your music notebook
when you finish. Happy hunting!

SECTION II   LET YOUR FINGERS DO THE WALKING:
                                     PIANO KEYBOARD

Please circle or write in your correct answers:

The piano keyboard has

a. 66   b. 77   c. 88 keys.

Some of the keys are white and some of the keys are

a. red   b. black.

There are more

a. white   b. green

keys than there are black keys.

Which of the following pictures shows the correct grouping of black keys?

a ‖ ❘ ‖ ❘   b ‖‖ ‖ ‖‖ ‖   c ‖‖‖ ‖ ‖‖‖ ‖

Play a key on the extreme left end of the keyboard.

The sound that you hear is

a. bright   b. dark.

The sound that you hear is

a. low   b. high.

The sound that you hear is

a. light   b. heavy.

What color or colors would best represent the quality of the sound that you
hear?   WHY?

Play a key on the extreme right end of the keyboard.

The sound that you hear is

a. bright   b. dark.

The sound that you hear is

a. low   b. high.

The sound that you hear is
a. light   b. heavy.

What color or colors would best represent the quality of sound that you hear?   *WHY?*

Now let's play the piano! Create the picture of clouds floating by on a beautiful spring morning. Which end of the keyboard did you use?   *WHY?*

Now create the picture of a loud, crashing, destructive thunderstorm. Which end of the keyboard did you use?   *WHY?*

Could you have used both ends of the keyboard for both pictures? EXPLAIN.

SECTION III   FAT, SKINNY, TALL, SHORT:
PIANO STRINGS!

Be brave! Take the top off the piano and peek inside! Along the back side of the piano you see a series of *strings*. These strings are made of
a. hair   b. wood   c. metal.

All the strings are attached to *knobs* that are made of
a. wood   b. metal   c. glass.

To tune the strings inside a piano, the piano tuner turns these knobs or *pegs* until the proper pitch is obtained.

While looking inside the piano, play a key on the extreme left end of the keyboard. Find the string that was struck when you played the key. Now play a key on the extreme right end of the keyboard. Find the string or strings that were struck when you played the key. Are the strings for both keys that you played the same *thickness*? Which string is the *thickest*?
a. the string for the dark sound?
b. the string for the bright sound?

Are the strings for both keys that you played the same *length*? Which string is the *longest*?
a. the string for the dark sound?
b. the string for the bright sound?

As you play the keys from the left end of the keyboard to the right end of the keyboard, you discover that the strings become:
a. thinner   b. thicker
            and
a. shorter   b. longer.

As the sounds become *higher* and *brighter,* the strings become:
a. thinner   b. thicker
            and
a. shorter   b. longer.

As the sounds become *lower* and *darker,* the strings become:
a. thinner   b. thicker
            and
a. shorter   b. longer.

Create the sound of an elephant walking! Which end of the keyboard did you use?   WHY?

Create the sound of birds singing! Which end of the keyboard did you use? WHY?

Could you have used both ends of the keyboard for *both pictures*? *Explain!*

SECTION IV   THE STRUCK AND THE STRIKER:
                                             STRINGS AND HAMMERS!

As you look inside the piano, play any key on the keyboard. Observe carefully what happens. When you play a key on the keyboard, a *hammer* hits the string (or strings) for the key that you played. Look at a hammer carefully. The hammer is made of

a. plastic   b. wood   c. metal   d. glass.

If the hammer were made of metal, would the sound be different?   WHY?

Draw a picture of a hammer right here!

While looking inside the piano, play the last key on the left end of the keyboard. This key produces the darkest, lowest sound on the piano. The hammer for this key strikes

a. 3 strings   b. 1 string   c. 5 strings.

The string for the darkest, lowest sound is generally

a. long   b. short.

While looking inside the piano, play the last key on the extreme right end of the keyboard. This key produces the brightest, highest sound on the piano. The hammer for this key strikes

a. 2 strings   b. 1 string   c. 3 strings.

The strings for the brightest, highest sounds are

a. thick   b. thin.

The strings for the brightest, highest sounds are

a. long   b. short.

As you play the keys on the keyboard from the left end of the keyboard to the right end of the keyboard, the number of strings for each key

a. decreases   b. increases.

SECTION V   FAR RIGHT PEDAL!

The *pedals* are located below the keyboard near the bottom of the piano. The piano has

a. 4   b. 1   c. 3

pedals.

The pedals are made of
a. wood   b. plastic   c. metal   d. glass.

Now look inside the piano. There are feltlike *dampers* touching most of the strings. Press down the far right pedal. When you press this pedal the dampers move
a. toward the strings   b. away from the strings.

While you have the far right pedal pushed down, play any key on the keyboard and listen carefully. Does the sound go away immediately or does it last for some time?

When you press down the far right pedal, the strings vibrate for
a. a longer period of time
b. a shorter period of time.

Look inside the piano again. Press down the far right pedal. Now play another key on the keyboard. Release the pedal. What happened to the sound when you released the pedal?

When you release the far right pedal, the dampers are moved
a. away from the strings
b. so that they touch the strings.

Releasing the far right pedal completely
a. stops   b. starts
the sound.

Now let's create a picture in sound! Press down the far right pedal again. *Play all the keys on the keyboard, one at a time, while holding down the far right pedal.* Is the sound that you hear clear or muddy?   *WHY?*

This type of sound could represent which of the following?
a. a murder   b. a clear mountain stream.

List three more pictures that this sound could represent!

SECTION VI   FAR LEFT PEDAL!

Look inside the piano. Now press down the far left pedal. When you press the far left pedal all the hammers inside the piano automatically move
a. away from the strings
b. closer to the strings.

Play any key on the keyboard. Press down the far left pedal and play the same key again.

When the far left pedal is pressed, the sound produced is
a. louder   b. softer.
WHY?

Why do you think the far left pedal is necessary?

SECTION VII   CREATING: LOOSE ENDS!

Draw a picture showing sound production of the piano from the playing of the key to the actual sound that is heard. Don't try to be Van Gogh—just be yourself!

You have learned that one usually plays the piano by using fingers on the keyboard. Now find other ways of producing sounds on the piano other than the usual way. Describe each way briefly in this space provided!

Make up a short original story! Use these unusual ways of playing the piano to help tell your story. Write your story on this page and show where each unusual method of sound production would be used in the story.

SECTION VIII   REVIEW: IT'S FUN TO RECAP!

Note to the teacher: At this point in the project I had available a list of review questions. Any method of review could be used. Follow-up could also include recorded listening to prepared piano pieces.

The next example is a short-term "mini-packet" that could be completed during one or two class periods. It was developed for intermediate levels (nine- and ten-year-olds). The song "I'm On My Way" would be available on a song sheet and also recorded on tape. As they begin, students should have the instruction sheet (reproduced below) and access to all materials called for. (The instructions could be recorded thus avoiding a reading problem for some students.) Before attempting this lesson, basic instruction on both autoharp and ukulele would also be necessary.

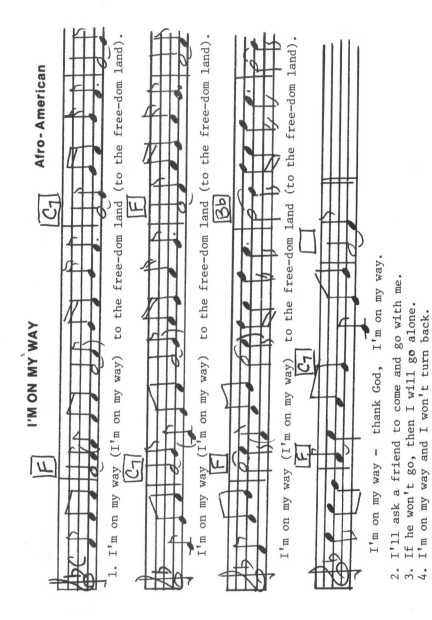

Figure 3-2

MINI-MUSIC PACKET

"I'm On My Way . . . Playing and Singing"

(Intermediate Level)

Goals: To describe what "call and response" means in music; to distinguish chord changes in a simple three-chord song; and to improve skill in playing the autoharp and uke.

To Get Ready: Get the song sheet for "I'm On My Way" (Figure 3-2) from the library center. Sign out a cassette recorder and the tape "I'm On My Way." Also sign out an autoharp and uke. As you finish each step in this packet, check the circle.

Start: Look through the song "I'm On My Way." It is a "call and response" song. Why? Write below.

Listen to the recorded song and follow the notes and words on the song sheet. Sing along on the "response" parts.

In the squares above the staff there are letter names for the chords that accompany the tune. Find these chords on the autoharp (F-C7-Bb). Strum each chord to get the feeling of changing from one to the other. Now practice them in the order they appear in the song: F-C7-F-Bb-F-C7-?. You found out the last square was blank, didn't you? Check each chord. Which sounds best? Write it in the square.[4]

Practice playing the chords as you sing the song. (You may ask a friend to sing along with you.) Record your performance on your own cassette.[5]

Practice the same chords on the uke. Tuning: G-C-E-A. Bb is a new chord, so practice finding it several times. Ask for help.

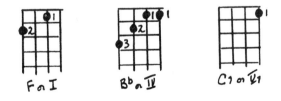

F a I   Bb a IV   C7 a V7

---

[4]Answer is "F."

[5]Each child has his own cassette tape in many open classrooms. It is used to record original compositions, performances, and other musical experiences in the same way a student notebook would be used in social studies.

Record your performance of singing and playing on the uke. Listen to both recordings—the one using the autoharp and the one using the uke. What could you do to improve each performance?

Circle the instrument you enjoyed the most.

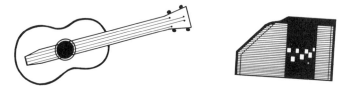

The last example of a learning packet at the early primary level consists of recorded instructions and four pages of response sheets. This packet, called "Freddie and the Bird," begins with a dramatic idea in poem and picture form and moves logically to abstract sound. The musical goals relate to high versus low sounds, and the responses called for are nonverbal. The sounds of the bird and the frog were made with a small bird whistle and a low, froglike vocal sound made by a man. Similar packets could be developed for the concepts of fast-slow; loud-soft; same-different; higher than-lower than; and so on.

The script should be recorded on tape by the teacher. The children would be provided with four response sheets (reproduced at the end of the script). They may listen in groups at a station or individually at one recorder.

MUSIC LEARNING PACKET[6]

"Freddie and the Bird"

(Early Primary Level)

Goal: The student will be able to distinguish between high and low sounds by drawing a circle around the correct symbol when he hears the sound.

Recorded on cassette by the teacher: "Look on *page 1* [see Figure 3-3] at the picture of the bird and the frog. Listen:

Freddie the frog
Sat on a log
Wishing he could sing like a bird.

---

[6]Developed in a graduate class in primary music, Georgia State University, Atlanta.

While up in the sky
A bird flew by
Tweeting a merry tune.
Said Freddie to the bird,
"The sweetest sound I've heard
'Tis the song you sing now."
[_____high sound on tape]
"Try as I might
My song is a fright
Listen to the song I sing."
[_____low sound on tape]
"But your song's too low
And could never go
As high as I sing now."
[_____high sound on tape]
"Then you sing high
And I'll sing low
Together on our way we'll go."
[_____high and low sounds
together on tape.]

"Let's listen to the sound of Freddie the frog and his friend the bird. This is Freddie the frog's low sound_____. This is the bird's high sound_____. Can you tell me who this is?_____.

"Turn to page 2."

Page 2

"Look at the top box of sets. Put your finger on the first set in the top box. Now you are ready to listen to this sound. _____. Is it a sound like Freddie the frog or a sound like the bird? Now circle the picture of the one you hear.

"Move your finger to the next set. Listen to the sound. If it is a high sound, circle the bird. If it is a low sound, circle Freddie.

"Repeat these directions for the rest of the page."

Page 3

"Look at the top box of sets. Put your finger on the first set in the top box. Now you are ready to listen to this sound._____. Is it a sound like Freddie the frog or a sound like the bird? Now circle the picture of the one you hear.

"Move your finger down to the middle box. Now point to the first set of circles. Listen to the sound of Freddie the frog. This time you will mark the bottom circle to show his low sound. Listen!—Now mark! Move to the next set of circles. Now listen to the high sound of the bird. Mark the top circle to show the high sound of the bird.

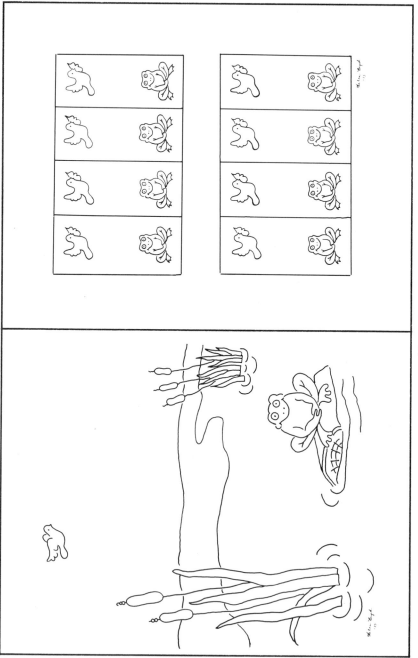

Figure 3-3

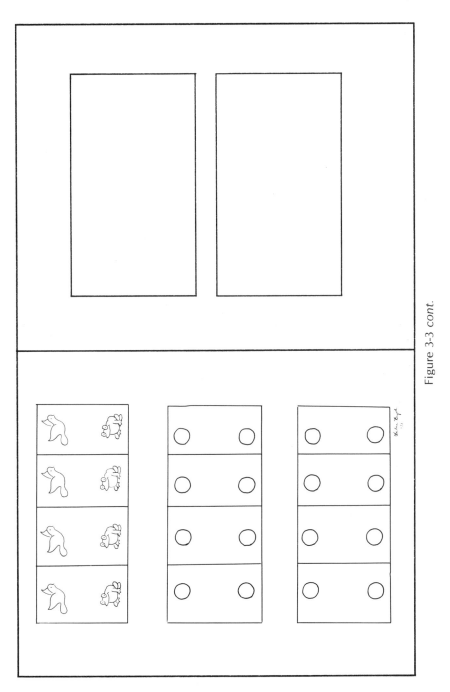

Figure 3-3 cont.

"Move to the next set of circles. Listen to the sound. If it is a high sound mark the top circle. If it is a low sound mark the bottom circle.

"Repeat for the bottom box of sets."

Page 4

"Now that you know the difference between a high sound and a low sound, let us find some things around the room that make high and low sounds. When you have found these things, come back to page 4 and draw those things that make high sounds in the top box, and the things that make low sounds in the bottom box. Before you begin to look for these sounds around your room, please turn off the tape recorder. Then, when you have finished finding them and drawing them in the correct boxes, turn the tape back on for more instructions.

"Now push the record button and record your high sounds and then your low sounds together. Tell me which are your high sounds. Tell me which are your low sounds."

Small-group Activities

Music programs may be individualized by using several types of small-group activities, usually going on at the same time within a given space. This type of multiple-activity approach was used experimentally in what is called the "Middle Learning Level" (ages nine to eleven) at the Galloway School in Atlanta.[7] Three of the activities are described below. They were presented to the children in ways consistent with the activity, that is, by demonstration as in the stick game; through teacher participation and follow-up "action" card as in the listening activity; or by simple teacher direction as in the sound mobile.

These could be thought of as open-ended experiences having many extensions. Observations and follow-up ideas are included after each activity providing a clue as to how the teacher evaluated them.

ACTIVITY #1: (4-6 students)

  I. Goals:
    A. To develop specific psychomotor responses to selected meter patterns.
    B. To create new psychomotor responses to selected meter patterns.

---

[7]These activities were developed by Paula Keller with the cooperation of Jeanette Lang, music teacher, Galloway School, Atlanta. The work of both of these teachers is gratefully appreciated by the author.

II. Materials:

Record player.

Selected recordings.

Several pairs of 8-9 inch lengths of broom handle or doweling (3/4" to 1" in diameter).

III. Procedures:

A. 1. Teacher explains and demonstrates a stick tapping game accompanying the four-beat piece of music. (Partners sit on the floor facing each other with a stick in each hand. First beat: tap end of sticks on floor. Second beat: hit crossed sticks. Third beat: toss-catch right-hand sticks to opposite partner. Fourth beat: hit crossed sticks. (Repeat.)

2. Students select from provided recordings and practice the stick game.

3. Students create new "moves" or patterns for the game.

B. 1. Teacher asks for volunteers from the participants to devise a less complex form of this game for younger children.

2. Students reinvent the game.

3. Students teach the new game to younger children.

IV. Observations and Follow-up Ideas:

A popular activity—many selected it. There were many ingenious ideas for variations of tapping and throwing the sticks. For a while, four students worked together, each with only one stick (because there were not enough to go around).

Only a few individuals had sufficient motor control to stay "with the beat" for very long. However, all observed tempo changes.

Group #1—Some argument over selection of music. Two girls returned to class because they wanted more variety in the music. Group #2—One boy got bored after a short while and switched to the sound sculpture group.

Second stage: Game for younger children: Four girls agreed to do this but were quickly tired of the simpler motions they needed. Used children's songs from MMYO, II, and employed slow *rolling* of sticks back and forth instead of throwing. Will teach it to four younger children next session.

ACTIVITY #II: (2-6 students)

I. Goals:

A. To exhibit perceptive listening with a selected piece of music.

B. To express the perceived elements of the music (1) nonverbally, (2) verbally, (3) visually.

C. To create a "sound" study or composition similar to the piece heard.

II. Materials:

Record player with 2-6 sets of headphones.

Selected recordings.
Drawing or painting materials.
Various melody and rhythm instruments.

III. Procedures:
  A. (Teacher-presentation)
    1. Teacher listens, with headphones, to a piece of music and describes it nonverbally to a group of students (gestures, rhythm patterns, facial expressions).
    2. Students guess, from several examples, which piece the teacher was listening to.
    3. Teacher and students discuss how and why the piece that was nonverbally described could or could not be recognized.
  B. (Partner-Experience Written on an "Action" or "Job" Card)
    1. With a friend, choose any record you like.
    2. Listen to it together, using earphones.
    3. As you listen, face each other and "tell" each other what you are hearing, *without using words*.
    4. After the music has ended, talk about it. Explain why you used certain actions or signs to describe it.
    5. Write a paragraph describing the music, or draw a picture about it.
  C. Students may elect to create a sound-study, using a variety of instruments, which is "like" the piece they described.
  D. If they wish to preserve their composition, they may notate, diagram, or record it.

IV. Observations and Follow-up Ideas:
  With both groups the teacher neglected to specify that the students were to deal with *only one* piece of music. Consequently, students listened to whole albums and did not proceed as expected. Both groups chose the Beatles' *Abbey Road* and were obviously enjoying their listening so much that the teacher did not stop them for concentration on one song.

  Group #1: Two rather quiet girls participated. They were completely uninhibited in nonverbal body motions. They agreed to return to the next session and narrow their listening to a favorite song from this album and to finish other steps of the activity. After they have finished with this, the teacher will ask them to try to process in describing a purely instrumental selection.

  Group #2: Six students. Showed no desire to interpret with body motions. However, when provided with paper and magic markers, they drew visual impressions of the songs they were hearing. Drawings indicated perceptive listening in regard to lyrics and moods. Because of timing aspects, the teacher will not follow up with an instrumental piece, but this should prove fruitful in eliciting responses to purely musical elements, eliminating the factor of lyrics.

For practical reasons (available students and time), the teacher decided to omit the composition stage of this lesson and to try the same sort of composition approach with a new group, using a literary model instead of a musical one.

ACTIVITY #III: (4-6 students)

I. Goals:
   A. To exhibit aural and visual selectivity and creativity in arranging sound-producing objects.

II. Materials:
   Tree branch.
   A variety of sound-producing objects (can lids, shells, paper, bottle caps, etc.).
   Tools necessary to manipulate these objects (string, scissors, etc.).

III. Procedures:
   A. Teacher asks for volunteers to make a "sound sculpture" or "sound mobile" from a variety of objects. It should be both aurally and visually pleasing.
   B. Students create the "sculpture/mobile."

IV. Observations and Follow-up Ideas:
   Four to five boys in each group chose this activity. Instead of working as a group on an "art work," they tended to individually devise small, complex, sound-producing constructions. Some of these were quite ingenious. One boy in Group #1 was more interested in visual appeal than the others. He arranged the various constructions in a balanced way on the tree branch.

   Since interest seems to be with individual invention, and more with sounds than with visual appeal, try having these boys contract to construct original instruments. Later they may wish to use them to accompany songs they know or in a sound composition of their own.

   Group #1: Actual process of *completing* the sculpture seemed to elicit more judgment, rearrangement, where before there was more interest in random experimentation.

   Two boys contracted to construct instruments.

Contracts

Many teachers find that contracting (sometimes called bargaining) is an effective way to individualize instruction. The process is aimed at developing skills of self-motivation and independence in selecting a task and seeing it through to completion.

It would be difficult to describe the many forms that contracting has taken in the open classroom. Sometimes a prescribed number of points are accumulated by students who in the end are expected to meet point levels for evaluation purposes. In other cases, the points are not used, but students are expected to accomplish a certain number of experiences over a period of time. Contracts can be selected by students at random from behavior categories, especially if contracting is used extensively. In this way, teachers can specify that contracts must be elected from each category. These categories are:

> *Composition* — Original sound pieces, improvisation, arranging, music writing.
> *Performance* — Playing instruments, singing, conducting.
> *Analysis* — Listening, describing, evaluating.

The following are samples of contracts used with ten- to twelve-year-olds in an open music program. These contract-activities did not have a point system as part of the evaluation. The teacher evaluated each student's work in terms of quantity and quality. The responses and materials called for in the contracts were stored in the student's individual work folder and storage space. He presented his results in writing on the contract form shown in Figure 3-4. Any additional materials, such as compositions, recordings, or performance, were presented to the teacher (or professional aid) when the contract was completed. When applied, this contract approach was highly successful with all children enthusiastically and musically occupied.

INSTRUCTIONS TO THE STUDENTS:

First Step: Decide the contract-category you are going to work in—composition, performance, or analysis. Read through the ideas for that category and make a first and second choice. (Someone else may be using the equipment you need for your first choice.)

Second Step: Fill out a contract form and begin work.

Third Step: When finished with your work, complete the evaluation part of the form. If you have performances, recordings, or compositions to present, arrange this with the teacher.

Fourth Step: Put the completed form in your music folder and select a new contract. Congratulations!

MUSIC CONTRACT FORM

If you mess up this form, get another and start over. Help each other—ask for help—be a friend.

My Name Is _____

Date Today Is _____

I Have Decided To Do Contract Number_____ (Fill in the Number)

I Have Already Finished (Circle) 0 1 2 3 4 5 6 7 8   Contracts

I Plan To Finish This Contract By   (Date) _____

Use the space below for any written work required in your contract; you may also use the back of this paper. If you need more space to write, get a blank piece of paper and staple it to this sheet and mark it page 2. Try to remember to put your name on all papers.

Now that I am finished, I would rate my work on this contract as (Circle): EXCELLENT GOOD FAIR.

I would like to do this contract again (Circle):
YES   NO.

(Note: Actual Size, 8-1/2″ x 11″)

Figure 3-4

Contract Samples (10- to 12-year-olds)

Contract descriptions are easier to use when color-coded by categories and placed on separate cards. When listed on sheets of paper, students tend not to read all the way through the suggestions before making selections.

COMPOSITION: **Composing What You See or "Filmstrip Studio"**

Using a large piece of newsprint, draw a pattern or design that you feel you could "translate" into a musical sound picture. Explore instruments and other sounds to fit your design. (You may ask a friend to help you if you need to make more than one sound at a time.) Record your sounds and make sure your "sound" picture matches your "visual" picture. *Now* repeat your "sight" picture on a write-on slide and project it on the screen. Play your music at the same time. Ask for help if you get stuck.

COMPOSITION: **Writing Your Own Music or "Composer's Workshop"**

Find a friend to help you. Lead him by asking him to play some musical sounds with you. Try to get variety of textures such as rough sounds, ringing sounds, etc. Put your sounds in some order —first one and then the other. *Now* use a large piece of paper and write your own musical symbols and notation to fit your composition. You may want to record your sound piece to use as you invent your own musical notation. In that way you can listen to it over and over. Keep improving it as you go along. Be sure the sounds don't stay too much the same. Give your composition a name. (Use colors for your symbols if you wish to.)

PERFORMANCE: **Playing the Autoharp, Uke, or Guitar or "Harmony Hall"**

Using the instruction book and other song materials that have chord symbols, learn to accompany at least three songs on the autoharp, uke, or guitar. Use a total of at least four chords. Be able to strum using more than one rhythm pattern. Write down the titles of the songs you learn to accompany and the names of the chords.

PERFORMANCE: **Learning to Conduct or "The Concert"**

Rehearse and conduct two songs using a chorus of at least four other students. Perform your selection for the class. Ask another class member to write a review of your performance for the music class (or school) newspaper.

ANALYSIS: Musical Description or "The Musical Door"

Name as many kinds of doors as you can. Start with your door at home, church, school doors, ancient doors, bank doors, etc. Describe them to yourself. Draw some. Decide on one particular door. Perform that door by putting sounds together according to the patterns on the door, the size of the door, interesting features of the door. Record the sounds. Listen. Where did sounds repeat? When did they change? What musical ideas would give the best clues as to the kind of door you had in mind? How could you change your "sound" door? Improve it. Write answers on contract form.

ANALYSIS: Photographing Sounds or "The Musical Photographer"

Take four photos of things that are making sounds at the time you snap the picture. Write a description of the sounds you heard when you took the photo. Now, take one photo of something that does *not* make a sound. Do something so that it *does* sound. Write what you did to make it sound. Ask someone if you do not understand what to do. Do not take more than a total of five snaps with the camera! If you do, we will run out of film. (Note to Teacher: Use a Polaroid for this contract.)

Job or "Task" Cards

The use of descriptive, single-experience cards is another way of individualizing the music program. These "job" or "task" cards, as they are often called, can be planned in conjunction with, or as integral to, contracting, project work, or packets. The advantage of job cards is their flexibility and the short length of time for which they are designed. They can often fill out experiences for students who have completed other lessons, or serve as a remedial practice.

Reproduced below are three job cards representing a variety of types. Each is presented to the student on a large card, or an 8-1/2" x 11" piece of paper.

(8- to 10-year-olds)   **MUSIC JOB CARD**

(for two people)

Make up a short melody on these bells.   Remember it.

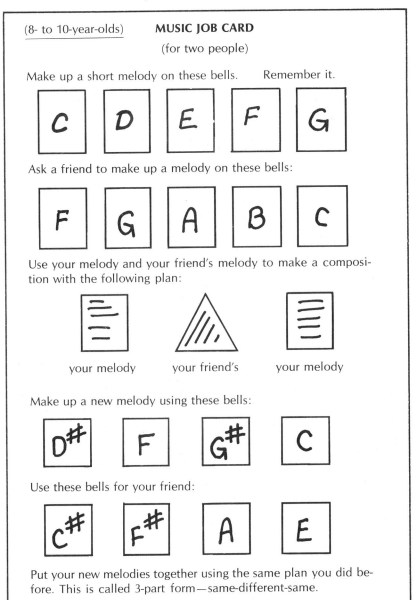

Ask a friend to make up a melody on these bells:

Use your melody and your friend's melody to make a composition with the following plan:

your melody   your friend's   your melody

Make up a new melody using these bells:

Use these bells for your friend:

Put your new melodies together using the same plan you did before. This is called 3-part form—same-different-same.

Which of the compositions is your favorite? Record it.

(10- to 12-year-olds)   **MUSIC JOB CARD**[2]

(for seven people)

Find these bells:

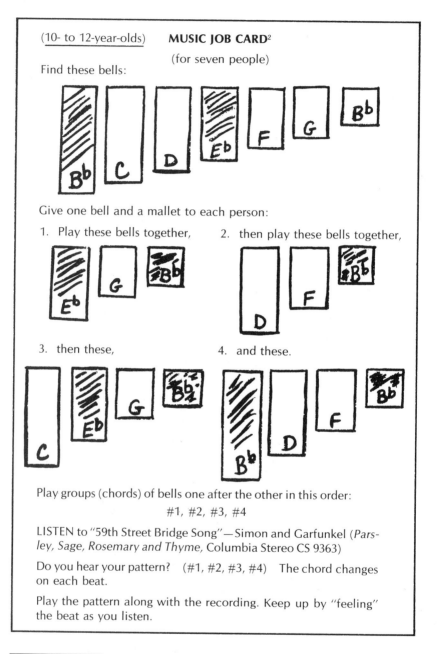

Give one bell and a mallet to each person:

1. Play these bells together,   2. then play these bells together,

3. then these,   4. and these.

Play groups (chords) of bells one after the other in this order:

#1, #2, #3, #4

LISTEN to "59th Street Bridge Song"—Simon and Garfunkel (*Parsley, Sage, Rosemary and Thyme,* Columbia Stereo CS 9363)

Do you hear your pattern?   (#1, #2, #3, #4)   The chord changes on each beat.

Play the pattern along with the recording. Keep up by "feeling" the beat as you listen.

[2] Prepared by Fred Willman, U. of No. Dakota. Used by permission.

MUSIC JOB CARD

Go to the listening center and find the recording of: *The Trout* in the *Bowmar Orchestral Library,* Number 83.[8] First you will hear a theme followed by six variations. As you listen to the music, circle the response you hear for each of the variations.

<u>Theme</u>: Simple Chordal Style

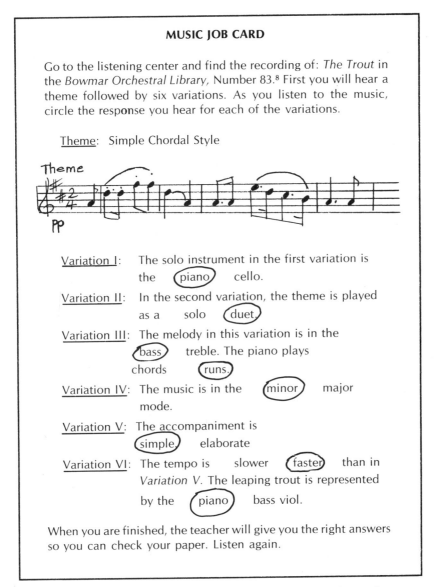

Variation I: The solo instrument in the first variation is the (piano) cello.

Variation II: In the second variation, the theme is played as a   solo   (duet.)

Variation III: The melody in this variation is in the (bass)   treble. The piano plays chords   (runs.)

Variation IV: The music is in the   (minor)   major mode.

Variation V: The accompaniment is (simple,)   elaborate

Variation VI: The tempo is   slower   (faster)   than in *Variation V.* The leaping trout is represented by the   (piano)   bass viol.

When you are finished, the teacher will give you the right answers so you can check your paper. Listen again.

Note: The correct answers are circled above. Also, students who attempt this job card should already be familiar with theme and variation form in music.

[8]Used by permission.

Useful Teaching/Learning Resources

A. *References for Reading and Research*[1]

Berg, Leila. *Look at the Kids.* Baltimore, Maryland: Penguin Books, Inc., 1972.

In a series of word pictures and photographs, the author acts out her title. Through anecdote and impression, with perception, compassion, and lyricism, these cameos show children in conflict with adults and their surroundings, and sometimes free to be themselves. The book engenders thought; it does not propose answers.

Brookover, Wilbur B. and Edsel L. Erickson. *Society, Schools and Learning.* Foundations of Education Series. Boston: Allyn and Bacon, Inc., 1969.

In presenting a sociological viewpoint of the school environment, historical and contemporary ideas about learning—and how certain of these ideas maintain dysfunctional aspects of the educational system—are examined.

The series of ideas includes how social forces influence student behavior, particularly learning behavior; how society is related to similar and different behavior in its individual members; the effects of subsocieties or subcultures (regional, rural-urban, ethnic, racial, and social-class); the effects of smaller groups and individual "significant others"; and the importance of self-perception in relation to others and society. A good resource for anyone contemplating curriculum change.

The Cutting Edge, Environmental Studies Project, Box 1559, Boulder, Colorado, 1972.

Contains accounts from about 100 teachers and students concerning their experiences with open education. Records successes and failures in helping learners grow. A good survey of ideas and suggestions for changing a classroom environment based on humanistic concepts of motivation and individual growth. Subtitled, "How to Innovate and Survive," the documents also include descriptive comments of teachers' moments of discouragement as well as elation. A must for those interested in open education.

---

[1] The author gratefully acknowledges the help of Mrs. Paula Keller in the preparation of these annotations.

Greer, Mary, and Bonnie Rubinstein. *Will the Real Teacher Please Stand Up?* Goodyear Education Series. Pacific Palisades, California: Goodyear Publishing Company, Inc., 1972.

A primer or "warm-up" for "getting with" concepts and techniques of open, humanistic education. The book consists of short articles, stories, poems, writings of both teachers and students, cartoons, photographs, suggested games and activities for the teacher or his students. Oriented to humanistic psychological premises, it deals with the student's viewpoint; the teacher, as a person and an educator; group relationships in exploring ideas and feelings; some current learning theories; and ideas about the future of education.

Hillson, Maurie, and Joseph Bongo. *Continuous-Process Education: A Practical Approach.* Palo Alto, California: Science Research Associates, Inc., 1971.

This book gives practical approaches for achieving continuous-process oriented education. It is a "how to" book with step-by-step suggestions drawn from the authors' experiences. The reader will learn how other educators, with a desire to individualize instruction and meet the varying requirements of students, have gone about the functions of curriculum planning, evaluating student needs, implementing programs, assessing and reporting student progress, and obtaining community support.

In assuming the need of many teachers for a simple, functional model, the authors have committed themselves to sequencing and the idea of levels, concepts that probably deserve additional examination and exploration.

Horton, John. *Music.* New York: Citation Press, 1972.

Developed in the context of the informal schools in Britain, this book demonstrates how music can form an integral part of the learning process by using choral singing, folk music, pop and classical music in conjunction with dance, drama, or social studies. Includes a seven-inch LP record with examples of music created by elementary children.

Hunter, Elizabeth. *Encounter in the Classroom.* New York: Holt, Rinehart, and Winston, Inc., 1972.

This book provides a simple and direct guide to necessary teacher behavior for a humanistic classroom environment. Activities are included that will help the teacher use encounter and sensitivity group techniques for increasing personal and interpersonal effectiveness. There are also "skill sessions" for analyzing and improving classroom talk, for improving the quality of classroom questions, and for helping teachers work more harmoniously with other adults. The thesis of the book is that possibilities inherent in any innovation in content or structure cannot be fully realized without accompanying changes in *process*.

Hurwitz, Emanuel, and Charles A. Tesconi, Jr., eds. *Challenges to Education: Readings for Analysis of Major Issues.* New York: Dodd, 1972.

This book presents a digest of significant writings about the relationships between school and society, focusing on fresh ideas about educational issues. Through an "issue-analysis" approach, articles about critical social-educational problems are examined by means of (1) description, (2) illustration, (3) analysis and (4) projection. Of special interest to students of open education are the chapters "The Relationship Between School and Society," "Students in Rebellion: Unrest in the Schools," "Ethnicity and the Schools," and "Alternatives to the Public School."

Kohl, Herbert R. *The Open Classroom.* New York: Vintage Books, A Division of Random House, Inc., 1969.

This handbook for teachers who want to work in an open environment is based on the author's experiences and those of other teachers. Though not a step-by-step program for change, it is basically about the battles with self and system that teachers encounter when they attempt to change traditional educational roles and practices. Kohl anticipates problems and makes suggestions that he hopes will be freely adapted. He presents strategies for change, for dealing with other teachers and administrators, for creating textbooks, lesson plans, etc., and provides illustrations from some classrooms in operation.

Lessinger, Leon M. *Every Kid a Winner: Accountability in Education.* Palo Alto, California: Science Research Associates, Inc., 1970.

This volume offers a clear formulation of what the author calls "educational engineering." This is a process that utilizes a wide variety of new technological and managerial resources to examine and change assumptions about education, ideas about aptitude, and expectations of educators, students, and the public. Its primary function is to provide accountability—for competence as well as cash. In focusing on the goal of guaranteed education for almost all children, the author discusses from a new perspective some of the ideas upon which open education is founded. His chief emphasis is on the means for implementing these and other innovations.

Marsh, Leonard. *Alongside the Child: Experiences in the English Primary School.* New York: Harper and Row, Publishers, 1970.

With reference to the modern English primary school, Marsh develops a "theory of education"—"theory" referring to what teachers know, believe, and feel about children as the determining factors in their daily actions. The school environment is seen as one planned to influence, to provide opportunities for choice within a carefully devised range, and to produce a climate where children experience a mature pattern of social relationships and catch a sense of standard and judgment in this pattern as well as in their work. A variety of open classroom ideas and approaches are clearly and delightfully presented. This book should prove extremely helpful to American teachers.

Marsh, Mary Val. *Explore and Discover Music.* London: The Macmillan Company, Collier-Macmillan, Ltd., 1970.

The author gives an account of her work with elementary and junior high school children, much of it in conversational form, documented with details of procedures, equipment, titles of music, and scores children themselves have created. Suggestions for promoting musical exploration and discovery are given throughout, along with discussions of related concepts and provisions for further exploration.

She offers a wealth of specific processes that can be helpful in the open classroom and are in complete accord with its underlying philosophies, i.e., "Creative thought and action flourish in an emotional climate that is relaxed and accepting of individual response, as opposed to an atmosphere that is rigid and demanding of conformity . . . Creativity is promoted by a rich environment of ideas, experiences, materials, and equipment."

Materials for Open Classroom. A "catalog-type" book with current materials and resources for open educational use. Well illustrated and useful, especially for classroom teachers. Available from Dell Publishing Co., 1 Dag Hammerskjold Plaza, New York, 10017.

"New Approaches to Music in the Classroom," *The Instructor* (April, 1972), 64-67.

A series of three concise and practical articles each written by an outstanding music teacher and edited by Elva S. Daniels. These articles could serve as guidelines for creative and expressive musical experiences consistent with the philosophy of open education. The ideas range from using word improvisations (Bert Kono-witz), to using physical space and providing proper environments (Barbara Hurley), and using ethnic as well as today's "pop" music (Peggy Zabawa).

Open Education: A Sourcebook for Parents and Teachers. Ewald B. Nyquist and Gene R. Hawes, eds. New York: Bantam Books, Inc., 1972.

In this comprehensive sourcebook, leading educators, psychologists, and authors present basic writings of the informal schooling movement that bears particularly on the American experience. Designed for practical use by all those who are interested in the introduction of open education into our schools, the book groups articles into major areas: I. "The Basic Differences and Advantages of Open Education," II. "How Open Education Functions," III. "Introducing Open Education into Schools," IV. "Basic Philosophy and Research Findings." A final section, including an annotated bibliography and other source listings, rounds off one of the most complete and thorough of available works about open education.

Renfield, Richard. *If Teachers Were Free.* New York: Dell Publishing Co., Inc., 1969.

Through vivid description of the hypothetical birth and development of Potseloo School, Dr. Renfield presents a logical discourse on the status, needs, and rationale for improvement in American schools. He challenges educators to pursue academic freedom, and to accept responsibility for demonstrating that their purposes, planning, and teaching have actually developed pupils' rational capacities. That development of the rational powers and values of the scientific spirit should be pursued as educational goals is an issue that is justified and examined in a framework consistent with current educational ideas.

Rogers, Carl R. *Freedom to Learn.* Columbus, Ohio: Charles E. Merrill Publishing Co., 1969.

Perhaps Rogers' most definitive book discussing the humanistic approach to teaching and learning, the first two sections of *Free-*

dom to Learn are practical, giving specific channels through which teachers may experiment. Section three provides some conceptual basis for such experimentation, and the fourth section gives personal and philosophical underpinnings and ramifications of the approach. Returning to practicality in the final section and epilogue, Rogers suggests a program for self-directed change. The addition of a well-annotated bibliography gives further sources for study of the humanistic approach.

Torrance, E. Paul. *Creativity.* What Research Says to the Teacher Series. Washington, D.C.: National Education Association, 1963.

The pamphlet draws from the findings of 500 research reports on creativity and attempts to show how these findings may help with the everyday problems of classroom teachers. The basic thesis is that many things can be learned more effectively and economically in creative ways, rather than by authority, and that this type of learning develops best under varied and informal conditions. Included are specific suggestions for what teachers can do to develop creativity in their classrooms and in themselves, and how certain common blocks to creativity may be overcome.

Toward Humanistic Education: A Curriculum of Affect. Gerald Weinstein and Mario D. Fantini, eds. New York: Praeger Publishers, 1970.

Weinstein and Fantini, directors of the Elementary School Teaching Project, and action-research program undertaken by the Ford Foundation's Fund for the Advancement of Education, present their major findings here. In attempting to discover successful teaching practices for ghetto children, they concluded that all children involve themselves in the learning process—regardless of age, socio-economic level, or cultural background—when this process relates to the affective or emotional life.

A forerunner of the current mass of humanistic and affective literature, this book represents itself as neither definitive nor complete, but as a practical, helpful beginning for the open-ended approach in teaching. Content includes analysis of the nature of instructional relevance, behavioristic goals, and relationships between the cognitive and affective domains. In addition, a detailed description of the ESTD model is presented.

B. *Instructional Resources for Individual and Small-group Work*[2]

Creating Music Through the Use of the Tape Recorder. A self-teaching color filmstrip prepared by Anne Modugno, and intended to involve the student in creative composition through the use of the tape recorder. Includes recording and teacher's guide as well as a booklet for the student. Order from Keyboard Publications, Inc., 1346 Chapel Street, New Haven, Connecticut 06511.

Do-It-Yourself Filmstrips. Twenty-five feet of blank, 35mm. film that will accept pen, pencil, or may be typewritten on. Can be erased or washed or made permanent with any spray-on coating. Includes indicators for frame lines and is perforated for use with any projector. Ten empty storage cans with labels and a set of felt-tip pens included ($13.00 per kit). Order from: Educational Activities, Inc., Box 392, Freeport, New York 11520.

Environmental Studies Kit. Consists of 75 assignment "experience" cards that are invitations to develop awareness and sensitivity to particular aspects of the self and the environment. Although not entirely devoted to music, there are several cards on sound, movement, and visual arts. The complete set includes a classroom wall chart for plotting student extensional activities. Applicable from the first grade through college, ($10.00 per set). Order from: American Geological Institute, Box 1559, Boulder, Colorado 80302.

Folk Songs of the World Series. A series of narrated recordings and accompanying filmstrips on the folk music of many countries keyed to the cultural, historical, and social life of the people. An excellent resource for the regular classroom program and easily adaptable to listening stations and centers. Catalog descriptions of these filmstrips and other resources in listening available from Bowmar Publishing Company, 622 Rodier Drive, Glendale, California 91201.

Jazz Greats—The Early Years. Six color filmstrips with captions telling the story of American jazz as it developed in its early years including the contributions of such musicians as W.C. Handy, Bessie Smith, Louis Armstrong, and "Jelly Roll" Morton. Order from: Educational Activities, Inc., Box 392, Freeport, New York 11520.

---

[2] In addition to the items listed here, the basic series texts are continually being revised to include a variety of instructional settings, notably individualized experiences in music.

Language Master. The *Language Master* is an individual learning machine unit often used in the teaching of language arts and can be adapted for music very easily. A stiff card with a strip of audio tape on it is inserted into a recording device. Students can record directly onto the card as they watch, or can listen to something that has already been recorded. Practice of pitch and rhythm patterns are common uses of the *Language Master.*

Learning to Play the Melodica. A self-instructional program written and privately available by writing to Professor Joe Baranko, Music Department, Alabama State University, Montgomery, Alabama.

Music Books for Young People, and *Developing Skills in Music.* These titles include several filmstrip sets on musical instruments, musical notation, and music reading. Recordings available. Catalog with details of these and other filmstrips available from Society for Visual Education, Inc., 1345 Diversey Parkway, Chicago, Illinois 60614.

The Music Box, by James R. Clemens. Musical activity box (like a recipe box) containing 150 cards for music making and learning. Includes games, holiday suggestions, and practice ideas for musical notation. Order from: Educational Insights, Inc., Dept. M-4., 423 South Hindry Avenue, Inglewood, California 90301.

Music 100 and *Music 300,* Brown-Troth. Two sets of narrated recordings with accompanying slides. *Music 100* consists of an introduction to music literature and history appropriate for young people. Excellent slides reinforce the stylistic characteristic of each musical period bringing in the principles of related arts as well. *Music 300* treats concepts of musical form and design. Both would be usable for individual work at the middle and upper levels. Order from: American Book Company, 300 Pike Street, Cincinnati, Ohio 45202.

Music Stories to Read and Hear (Reading Enrichment Program). A new series of eight interesting narratives on the music of various composers. Boxed with story cards, response-mechanisms for individual children, and a recording for each story. An excellent addition to the reading enrichment program available with records or cassettes. Order from: Keyboard Publications, Inc., 1346 Chapel Street, New Haven, Connecticut 06511.

Musimeasure (A Music Game). Created by Clifford Boatner, pianist and mathematics teacher. A card game consisting of nine time-signature cards. Game is based on the fact that numerical fractions can be combined to make full units; in music, fractional notes and rests can be combined to make up full musical measures. Available from the catalog: *Materials for Open Classroom,* Dell Publishing Company.

Pathways to Music Series and *Man and His Music Series.* Sets of multimedia kits including color sound-filmstrips (on record or cassette), study prints and teacher's guides. Excellent new titles include topics relating music with social studies such as "Challenge of China," "The Sounds of Africa," "The Message of Rock," and "Voices from the Middle East." Other titles with descriptions of music are found in the catalog of Keyboard Publications, Inc., 1346 Chapel Street, New Haven, Connecticut 06511.

Pipeline, Jane Beethoven, ed. A new monthly publication available by subscription. Includes currently popular music of famous and "recognizable" musical groups. Has multiple copies of well-illustrated reading and problem-solving materials together with a 45 rpm. recording. Order from: Silver-Burdett Publishing Co., (General Learning Corporation), Morristown, New Jersey.